Cool CARD TRICKS & GAMES

BOB LONGE & ALFRED SHEINWOLD

STERLING INNOVATION®
An imprint of Sterling Publishing Co., Inc.

New York / London
www.sterlingpublishing.com

STERLING and the distinctive Sterling logo are registered trademarks of Sterling Publishing Co., Inc.

2 4 6 8 10 9 7 5 3 1

Published by Sterling Publishing Co., Inc.
387 Park Avenue South, New York, NY 10016

This book is comprised of material from the following
Sterling Publishing Co., Inc. titles:
101 Best Card Games for Children by Alfred Sheinwold
© 1956 by Sterling Publishing Co., Inc.
The Little Giant® Book of Card Tricks © 2000 by Bob Longe

Clip art images © 2008 Jupiterimages Corporation

© 2008 by Sterling Publishing Co., Inc.
Distributed in Canada by Sterling Publishing
c/o Canadian Manda Group, 165 Dufferin Street
Toronto, Ontario, Canada M6K 3H6
Distributed in the United Kingdom by GMC Distribution Services
Castle Place, 166 High Street, Lewes, East Sussex, England BN7 1XU
Distributed in Australia by Capricorn Link (Australia) Pty. Ltd.
P.O. Box 704, Windsor, NSW 2756, Australia

Sterling ISBN 978-1-4027-6028-0

For information about custom editions, special sales, premium and
corporate purchases, please contact Sterling Special Sales
Department at 800-805-5489 or specialsales@sterlingpublishing.com.

CONTENTS

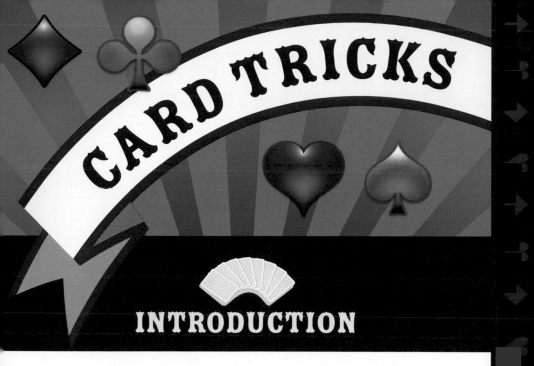

CARD TRICKS

INTRODUCTION

Most of the tricks in this book require little or no sleight of hand. But some truly marvelous tricks are available to those willing to master a few moves. I think you'll like the sleights presented here. They are useful, not only for the tricks in the book, but also for stunts of your own devising. For each move, you're offered alternatives, giving you the opportunity to choose one that appeals to you. Your best bet is to work on each sleight until you have mastered it—that is, until you can perform it effortlessly and undetectably.

If you're a beginning magician, I recommend that you practice the tricks. Connect your sequence in some way—perhaps a theme, or a story that will encompass all of them. I must admit, however, that some magicians—and very good ones at that—make no attempt to integrate their tricks; they simply proceed from one trick to the next. I don't recommend this to the beginner, but it might work well for you.

Be sure to save your best trick for last. When performing for friends, *quit* after doing your best trick. Even when they plead for more, don't make the mistake of performing some half-learned tricks that do not measure up.

Incidentally, I use a standard shorthand to signify the cards: 9H for 9 of hearts, KS for king of spades, 2C for 2 of clubs, and so on.

To all my readers, good luck and good magic.

Bob Longe

For purposes of discussion, we might divide every magic trick into two parts: the *secret* and the *presentation*.

The Secret

Too many beginning magicians (and, unfortunately, some of the more experienced) believe that once they have the secret to a trick, that's all there is to it. It's probably true that we all start out that way. We know the secret; they don't. So we fool people. But that isn't magic; that's a puzzle. "Na-na-na-na-na-nah! You don't know what I did."

Clearly, an important part of knowing the secret is making sure that others don't discover it. But if all you have is the unvarnished secret, many might very well figure out what the secret is. So let's move on to *presentation*.

The Presentation

We could divide this into unlimited categories, but let's make it three: entertainment, misdirection, patter. Yes, yes, I realize that there's considerable overlapping, but this division makes it easy to discuss the important points.

Each one of these categories can help disguise the secret.

Entertainment

If your trick has no point to it other than to display your skill or knowledge, why should anyone else be interested? The trick should also have an entertaining theme. Perhaps you're interested in displaying a curious mental phenomenon you've noted. Maybe certain cards seem determined to return to the top. Is it possible that the aces insist on being grouped together no matter how you separate them?

You find someone's chosen card. Not good enough! Instead, years ago a Hindu magician passed a mysterious power onto you that makes it possible for you, sometimes, to actually find someone's selected card.

But entertainment is more than just telling a story. It's developing a friendly attitude toward spectators. Your primary concern is that they should enjoy themselves. They're not saps or suckers, and you're not the wise guy who knows more than they do. You *and* the spectators should both be astonished at the miracles that keep happening.

To entertain, you must be properly prepared. Don't be like the jokester who forgets the punch line. You should know exactly what you're doing. If you seem to fumble, it's because you're doing it deliberately as part of the trick. In other words, you must practice, practice, practice if you intend to entertain.

Furthermore, be yourself. Don't be Mr. or Ms. Supermagician unless you can make it really comical. Whatever your personality is, let it shine through. My good friend Bobby Kelly performs tricks in a grand manner, because that's his natural way about everything. I, on the other hand, perform whimsically, even comically, because I see humor in almost everything. Consider David Copperfield; when he performs, he obviously enjoys himself. *He* is having fun, so the audience has fun as well. Perhaps there's a lesson there for all of us lesser lights.

Misdirection

Nearly all of magic depends on misdirection in one way or another. Some is subtle, and some is blatant. (Watch out! I'm about to divide things again.) For purposes of discussion, let's consider three categories of misdirection: time misdirection, physical misdirection, and verbal misdirection.

Time Misdirection

Time misdirection operates when you need the audience to cease concentrating on something or to forget precisely what has transpired, so you shift to something else for a while. It is used more frequently than you might think. For instance, you apparently place the JH into the center of the deck. You have performed the sleight necessary to keep the card on top or return it to the top. Do you show the card immediately? Of course not. Common sense tells you to separate the sleight from the denouement with a bit of time. You ask a spectator to tap the top card of the deck, or you announce, "I wonder if the jack of hearts will be content to remain way down in the deck." *Then* you show that the JH has returned.

You weren't even aware that time misdirection was involved; you were just building to a dramatic climax.

Time misdirection should be subtle. You shouldn't in effect say, "Let's wait a minute so that you can forget which pile is which." Instead, you might pause to stress the spectator's complete freedom of choice, or to point out that occasionally your mental powers help you to identify a chosen card. But whatever you do or say, the pause should have *some* relevance. There are many examples of time misdirection in this book. Notice how it improves some tricks, and how it is absolutely essential to others.

Physical Misdirection

The magician waves his right hand in the air. Everyone's eyes follow. Beware of what's going on with the other hand.

Your eyes are important when you are using physical misdirection. If you want the group to look at something, *you* look at it. If you want a spectator to stop staring at your hands, talk to that person and make eye contact.

Let's suppose you'd like to perform a secret operation with the deck. Nothing to it. Have a spectator choose a card. "Please show it around," you say. Turn your back so that you can't possibly catch sight of the card. And, while your back is turned, do your dirty work.

Verbal Misdirection

Years ago, a popular song was "It's a Sin to Tell a Lie." Most lying is still considered reprehensible—except lying by comics and magicians. Actually, it's expected of them. Comics lie to make their tales funnier; magicians lie to enhance their tricks.

"While traveling in the Orient," says the magician, who has never been more than fifty miles outside of Podunk, Michigan, "I discovered this magical vase." Actually, he ordered it from Abbott's in Colon, Michigan. But no one cares. The little lie adds a bit of romance to the trick.

But how do you misdirect verbally? Lying, as usual. There are many examples in this book, but let me provide an additional few. One of my earliest card inventions had certain weaknesses. One was that the spectator had to deal out a fairly large number of cards into a pile, thus reversing their order. Why should he do this rather than simply cut off a pile of cards? Maybe that will never occur to him. But to make sure it doesn't, I say, "I'd like you to deal these cards into a pile." The spectator deals out a fairly large number of cards. "Stop whenever you feel like it. The idea is that you deal the exact number of cards that you wish." Sure sounds fair, doesn't it?

This sort of verbal misdirection can often turn a weakness into strength.

Patter

We've divided magic tricks into two parts—the secret and the presentation. Under presentation, we looked at entertainment and misdirection. Now it's time for patter, which is the story that goes with the trick.

Suppose you're watching an illusionist on television. He is captured by mysterious medieval creatures who tie him up and place a hood over his head. He is led to an altar where he is to be slain. But, at the critical moment, the hood is removed from his head, and the person is *not* the magician. All the creatures fall back in amazement as their leader removes his mask and turns out to be the magician.

That's the story, the plot. And that's what makes the trick entertaining.

Using the identical plot, you could perform an intriguing trick with cards. In fact, now that I think about it, I may give it a shot one day.

The point? Dress up every trick with some kind of story or patter. The story can be silly, amusing, or—as above—rather serious. Practically everyone enjoys a good story. The story might be wildly fictitious, or it might be as simple as this declaration: "My Uncle Ed passed on to me this effect, and he made me promise never to reveal the secret. The only trouble is I've never been able to make it work. Well, here goes one more try."

For the tricks in this book, I've provided patter points. I highly recommend that you adopt the themes that you find worthwhile, but use your own words.

PEEKS

Quite often, for a trick to be successful you must secretly learn the name of the top or bottom card of the deck. Here are four excellent methods.

Easy Glimpse

A spectator has chosen a card, and you'd like to know the name of either the top or bottom card of the deck. Say to the spectator, "Show the card around, please."

Lower your head so that you're looking downward, presumably so that you won't inadvertently catch a glimpse of the selected card. And just to make sure, you briefly turn sideways to the group. You're holding the deck at your side in your left hand. Tilt the deck counterclockwise so that you can see the bottom card with a quick glance. (Since your head is already bowed, you need not move it.)

Turn back to the group and continue. If you wish to bring the card to the top, simply give the deck one overhand shuffle, taking off the last few cards one at a time. This brings the bottom card (which you know) to the top.

Shuffle Peek

You wish to know the top card of the deck. Hold the deck in your left hand in the overhand shuffle position. Your left side should be somewhat toward the spectators. As you reach with the right hand to begin the overhand shuffle, let the deck tilt back a bit in the left hand so that you catch a glimpse of the bottom card (as in the illustration).

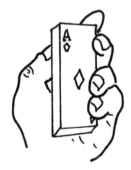

Shuffle the bottom card to the top, as described above.

Sneaky Peek

Here is an easy method to peek at the bottom card. Fan out a dozen or so cards from the top, taking them in your right hand. Hold them up so that spectators can see the faces but you can't. Turn your left hand over inward and run your left first finger from right to left behind the cards in a sweeping gesture, taking a quick peek at the bottom card of the deck (as in the illustration). As you perform the sweeping movement, comment, "You'll notice that the cards are really well mixed."

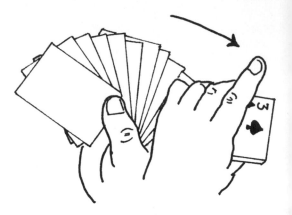

Turn the cards in your left hand face down and return the fanned cards to the top.

The Tilt Peek

Frequently, it's useful to glimpse the bottom card after taking the deck back from a spectator. Here is an excellent method.

Take the deck back with the palm-down right hand (as in the first illustration). Then tilt the deck clockwise as you transfer it to the palm-up left hand (as in the second illustration). Naturally, you peek at the bottom card as you tilt the deck.

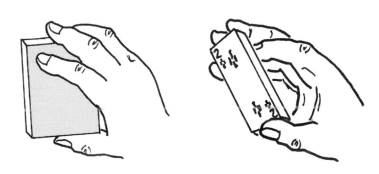

1

SLEIGHTS

FORCES

There are innumerable ways in which a card can be forced on a spectator. Forces can come in handy in a variety of tricks, but they are particularly useful in a mental routine. The performer announces, "I'd like someone to choose a card in a perfectly fair way. Then I'll try to read that person's mind." And, of course, the performer succeeds.

Certainly, the above is a better approach than simply having a card chosen and then naming the card. If nothing else, it gives you a chance to perfect your acting ability as you apparently strain your brain trying to identify the chosen card.

The forces that follow are standard and quite well known among magicians. This doesn't mean they aren't effective; that's how they get to be standard.

Crisscross Force

For this force, you must know the top card of the deck. A number of possibilities are presented under "Peeks," pages 11 to 12.

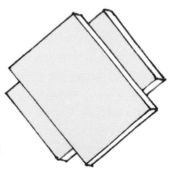

Set the deck onto the table. Ask a spectator to cut off a pile and place it on the table. Pick up the other pile and place it crosswise on the pile that was cut off. (Or you may have the spectator do this.)

The deck should look like the illustration.

Provide time misdirection by chatting with the spectator briefly. This should help everyone to forget the true relationship of the two piles.

Touch the top card of the lower pile, saying, "Please take a look at your card."

It is, of course, the original top card of the deck.

Easy Force

This Stewart James creation is one of the best nonsleight forces ever. As with the previous force, you must know the top card. An easy way to accomplish this is to fan through the cards, demonstrating that they are in no particular order. Or you might check out "Peeks," on pages 11 to 12.

Hold the deck in the dealing position in your left hand. Place your left hand behind your back. Bring your right hand behind your back and grip your left wrist, as in the illustration below. Address a spectator: "I'll turn my back to ensure that I have no way of controlling your choice." Turn your back to the spectators. Again, speak to the spectator: "Please cut some cards off the top of the deck, turn them over, and set them face up on top of the rest of the deck."

After the spectator finishes, face the group once more, saying to your assistant, "You had complete freedom of choice, right?" As you say this, lift off the top card of the deck with your right hand. Place your left thumb under the deck and flip it over as shown in the opposite illustration. Place the card that's in your right hand on top of those in your left hand. As you do this, pick up the entire deck with your right hand and bring it forward. The entire process should take no more than a few seconds.

The spectators will see on top of the deck the face-up card that was cut to. This should reassure those who are paying attention. Don't call attention to the card.

Fan through the face-up cards to the first face-down card. Lift off all the face-up cards and extend the face-down cards to the spectator, saying, "Please take a look at your card." It is, of course, the one you peeked at. Restore the deck to its proper order and proceed with your trick.

It might be worth your while to acquire the knack of doing the business behind your back with one hand. It will take considerable practice, however. You place only your left hand behind your back. After the spectator cuts off a pile and places it reversed on top of the remaining cards, you face the spectators. With your left thumb, you slide off the top card to the left and, at the same time, with fingers and thumb flip the deck over. The card is now on top of the original bottom portion.

As soon as the move is complete, bring the deck forward.

FALSE CUTS

Magicians often give the deck a false shuffle or a false cut to demonstrate that the cards are mixed. Most of the time, spectators have no reason to believe otherwise, so the shuffles and cuts serve only to create suspicion. Mind you, they can be essential to certain tricks; but they should be used sparingly.

Whatever the situation, perform these sleights *casually*.

Table Cut 1

Both of the false cuts in this section are of my own invention.

Hold the packet in the dealing position in your left hand. With your right hand, pick off about the top third of the packet. Place this group in front of you.

Cut off another third with the right hand and place this group *forward* of the first group.

Take the last third with your right hand and place it *forward* of the other two groups. The illustration shows the present position.

Pick up the group nearest you and place it on top of the middle group. Pick up the combined packet and place it on top of the farthest group. In that same movement, pick up the entire packet. Place the packet in the dealing position into your left hand.

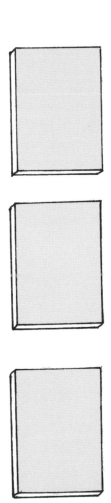

Table Cut 2

Again, hold the packet in the dealing position in your left hand. With your right hand, lift off about a third of the cards from the top of the pack, and place this group onto the table.

Cut off another third with the right hand and place it six to eight inches to the right of the first group.

Take the remaining group with your right hand and place it *between* the other two piles. The illustration above shows the current position.

With your right hand, pick up the pile on the right; at the same time, with your left hand, pick up the pile on the left. Place the group in your right hand on top of the middle pile; immediately place the group in your left hand on top.

Pick up the entire packet with your right hand and place it in the dealing position into your left hand.

Both this and the previous cut should be done fairly rapidly and certainly with no hesitation.

THAT CERTAIN FEELING

A Fine Touch

Sometimes a minor error works in your favor. Milt Kort showed me a trick he ascribed to Stewart James. The next time I saw him, Milt told me that he had misremembered the James trick and, as a result, had shown me a similar trick that apparently he had invented on the spot. It was too late, however. I had already worked out a simpler handling and was having great success with the misremembered effect—the one I'm about to describe.

The trick is extremely simple, but because of the presentation is also very deceptive.

For the present trick, all you need do is get a peek at the bottom card and remember it. (See "Peeks," on pages 11 to 12.) Set the deck face down onto the table. Ask your assistant, whom we'll call Madeline, to cut the cards into three piles, about equal. You know the bottom card of one of the piles, so you'll make sure Madeline chooses that particular one.

"Madeline, I'll pick a pile, and then you pick a pile." Pick up a pile other than the one with the card that you peeked at. "Now your turn."

She picks up one of the remaining two piles. If it's the one that has the known bottom card, fine. Pick up the one remaining on the table and turn your back.

If she picks up the other pile, hold out your hand, take the pile from her, and turn your back.

If she is not holding the pile in her hand, have her pick it up from the table. With appropriate pauses, direct Madeline: "Pick up your pile, please. Hold it face down, fan through it, and take out any card you wish. Look at it and remember it. Now put that card *face up* on top of the pile. Give the pile a complete cut so that your card ends up somewhere in the middle."

The illustration below shows the position as though the cards were fanned out.

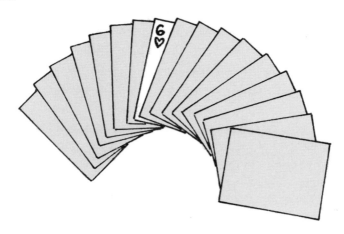

When Madeline is done, turn back to the group. Set the cards you're holding onto the table. Take the packet from Madeline and put it behind your back.

"Through sense of feel alone, Madeline, I'm going to find the card you chose, and I'll also name it."

Riffle through the packet fairly noisily. "Okay, I've found your card. At least I think so." Pause. "Madeline, you chose a very difficult card. I just can't seem to distinguish it from others like it. Maybe . . ." Pause. "Yes, maybe I can figure out the name of the card that's facing it."

Name some distinguishing feature of the card you peeked at, like, "Yes, it's a face card," or, "It seems to be a black spot card." Eventually, name the card that you peeked at. Suppose that the card is the 6S. Say, "The card is the six of spades. Yes, six of spades. That's the card that's facing your chosen card." You want to make that part perfectly clear.

Bring the cards forward and fan down to the face-up chosen card. Remove it and the card facing it. Set the rest of the packet aside. Noting the face-up card, comment, "No wonder I couldn't figure out what card it was. I kept confusing it with . . ." Name a similar card or two.

"I said that the card facing yours is the six of spades. Let's see if I'm right." Turn the other card face up, revealing the one you named.

MENTAL TRICKS

The beauty of mental magic is that there is a certain logic to it. How did you discover the name of the card? Not by treachery or deceit—oh, no! You read the person's mind.

Did you in some despicably sneaky way force the selection of a card, so that you knew the name of the selection in advance? Certainly not. You concentrated, hoping that your special ESP gift would somehow convey to you the name of a selection in advance; then you made your prediction.

For a number of reasons, playing cards are perfect for mental magic. For instance, practically any method of forcing a card can be used for either mind reading or prediction. Furthermore, predictions are easily made since you don't need pencil and paper; all you need do is set aside (face down) a card that is the same value and suit as your force card and announce that it is your prediction.

When you're mind reading, cards provide dramatic denouements as you gradually reveal color, suit, and value.

Your Favorite Card

I recently concocted this easy prediction trick, which has proven very effective.

Hand your assistant Evan the deck. As you do so, ask, "What's your favorite card?" He tells you, and you make a mental note. "Give the cards a shuffle, please."

Take the deck back and say, "I'll have to find a prediction card." Let's suppose that Evan's favorite card is the QS. Hold the cards with the faces toward yourself and fan through them, looking for the QS. When you find it, count it as one as you move it into the right hand with the others. Continue counting until you reach ten. After transferring card number ten to your right hand, cut the cards at that point, thus bringing the QS to the position of tenth from the top.

As you cut the cards, say, "Can't seem to find a good prediction card."

Start fanning the cards from the bottom again. Note the tenth card from the bottom. Continue fanning through the deck until you find the card that matches it in color and value. (Make sure you don't take it from the top ten cards.) If the appropriate match is among the bottom ten or the top ten, just remove a card of the same value. Place this card onto the table, announcing that it's your prediction.

Hand the *face-up* deck to Evan. "Please deal the cards into a face-up pile, Evan." Make sure he doesn't turn the deck face down before he starts dealing. After he has dealt 15 cards or so, say, "You can stop whenever you want."

When he stops, have him turn the dealt pile face down. For explanatory purposes, I'll call this Pile 1. Meanwhile, Evan is holding most of the deck, still face up in his left hand. "Turn the cards you're holding face down, Evan. In a moment I'll turn away. After I do, I'd like you to move some cards from the top of that pile to the bottom. Why don't we do it this way? Think of a number from one to seven, and move that many cards from the top to the bottom. Tell me when you're done."

Turn away while he performs his task.

When you turn back, pick up the packet that remains on the table. "We want to make sure that we select a card completely by chance, Evan. Now what's your favorite card?"

He names it again.

"Let's each deal our cards face up into a separate pile. We'll do it together." You each deal a card face up into a pile. You each deal another, and continue until Evan turns up his favorite card, the QS. You both stop dealing immediately.

"So there's your favorite card. Now what was the number you thought of, the number from one to seven?" He names it. Let's suppose he names the number five. You count aloud as you deal one less than that number face up onto your pile. In this instance, you would deal four cards face up onto your pile. Take off the next card, saying, "Five." Without letting anyone see its face, place it next to your prediction card.

Before proceeding, gather all the other cards into one face-down pile. This makes for a cleaner climax.

"So we've chosen a card using your favorite card and a number you've selected at random. If we're *extremely* lucky, maybe your selection will match my prediction. And vice versa."

Turn the two cards over at the same time, showing that they actually do match.

It's a Setup!
Stewart James invented an intriguing prediction trick using dominoes. I have adapted the trick to playing cards and have tossed in a few ideas of my own.

In advance, stack nine cards on top of the deck. From the top down, these are the values; the suits are irrelevant:

8 A 6 3 5 7 4 9 2

If you can, give the deck a false shuffle or a false cut, retaining the position of at least the top nine cards.

Say, "I'll need to find a prediction card."

8	A	6
3	5	7
4	9	2

Fan through the deck with the faces of the cards toward yourself, apparently looking for a prediction card. Actually, you're counting the cards. Note the fifteenth card from the bottom. Go through the rest of the deck to find the card that matches this in color and value. Remove this card from the deck and set it aside face down, announcing that it's your prediction card. Make sure you don't take this card from the bottom fifteen cards, or from the top nine. If you can't find the exact mate, simply take out a card of the same value. (Occasionally, all the other possibilities will be among the bottom fifteen or the top nine. When this occurs, chances are a matching card will be among the bottom fifteen. Take a card from the rest of the deck, study it, shake your head no, and replace the card among the bottom fifeen. Study the cards further. Finally remove the appropriate matching card from the bottom fifteen and place it onto the table.)

Set the deck down, saying, "I've made my prediction; I won't touch the deck again."

Ask your assistant Rose to help out. "Please pick up the deck, Rose. Now you're going to get a choice. You can either deal cards face down from the top of the deck, or you can turn the deck over and deal them face up from the bottom. Which will it be—top or bottom?"

Let's suppose she chooses to deal from the bottom. Say, "Please turn the deck over, Rose, and deal the cards into a pile."

Make sure she has dealt several cards past fifteen before you say, "Stop whenever you wish."

When she stops, ask her to turn the pile face down.

"Rose, we're going to choose a number down in that pile in the fairest possible way. Turn the cards you're holding face down. Deal the top three cards into a face-down row, going from left to right. Below them, deal the next three out in the same way. Below that last three, deal three more in the same way."

The face-down cards will be as shown on the opposite page. Notice that the values are shown for clarity, but the cards are actually face down, and they form a so-called "magic square": Each row, each column, and each diagonal add up to fifteen.

"Please set the rest of the cards you're holding over here." Indicate a position some distance from the pile she dealt out from the bottom. "Now I'd like you to choose any row or any column." As you say this, with your finger indicate first the rows and then the columns. "In fact, you can choose either of the diagonals." With your finger, indicate the two diagonals.

Pass your finger over the rows, columns, and diagonals as you say, "You have one, two, three, four, five, six, seven, eight possible choices. Which do you select?"

When she indicates her choice, have her turn over the appropriate three cards. "Add those up, please, Rose. What do you get?"

She tells you fifteen.

"Please pick up the other pile and deal off fifteen cards into a pile."

After she deals off the fifteen cards, tell Rose, "Please turn over the last card you dealt." She does. "Now pick it up and show it around, please." As she does this, gather up *all* the other cards on the table except for the prediction card. Casually give these cards a little shuffle as you say, "Would you please turn over my prediction card to see if there's a match?" She does, and there is.

But let's go back. What if Rose decides to deal from the top? Surely you've figured it out already. If she deals from the top, she deals the top three cards into a row, the next three into a row beneath them, and the last three into another row.

As before, you tell her, "Please turn the deck over, Rose, and deal the cards into a pile."

She should deal several cards past fifteen before you say, "Stop whenever you wish."

When she stops, ask her to turn the pile face down.

Then it's back to the nine cards. And the conclusion follows, as described above.

MENTAL COMPETITION

In this trick, you apparently match wits with spectators, giving them a fair chance to defeat you. Actually, because of your superior intellect (and low animal cunning), you invariably emerge victorious.

Odds and Evens

Your friend Barney will bet on almost anything. Perhaps this will teach him a lesson. "Barney, I'd like to make a wager with you, but not with real money. Here it is: I'd like you to cut the deck into five piles. Chances are, some piles will contain an even number of cards, and others will contain an odd number of cards. I'll bet that an *odd* number of piles will have an *even* number of cards.

"In other words, I win if *one* pile contains an even number of cards and the other four contain an odd number; I win if *three* piles have an even number of cards and the other two have an odd number; and I win if all *five* piles hold an even number of cards.

"So I bet that an *odd* number of piles will have an *even* number of cards. Otherwise, you win."

Reflect a moment.

"It seems to me that the odds are a little in my favor. If we were actually betting, I probably should give you two-to-one odds. Or, even better, five-to-one odds. I couldn't give a better deal to my own brother."

Evidently, you're not very nice to your own brother. You could give whatever odds you wish; you will *always* win the bet.

Barney cuts the cards into five piles. Have him do the counting. He counts one pile. If the pile contains an odd number of cards, he places the pile near him; if it contains an even number of cards, he places it near you. This makes it easy to see that you are the winner.

I suggest you do it only one more time. More than that and even Barney may suspect that he doesn't stand much chance.

Note: Make sure you're using a complete fifty two–card deck. Otherwise, you might lose. The stunt works with any *even* number of cards.

GO FISH

Number of players: three to five

The Object of the Game
To form more "books" than any other player. A book in this game is four of a kind, such as four kings, four queens, and so on.

The Deal
If only two play, deal seven cards to each player. If four or five play, deal five cards to each. Put the rest of the pack face down on the table, forming the stock.

The Play
The player to the dealer's left begins. Let's say that's you. You say to some other player, "Jane, give me your 9s." You must mention the name of the player you are speaking to (Jane), and you must mention the exact rank that you want (9s), and you must have at least one card of the rank that you are asking for (9) in your hand.

The player you are speaking to (Jane) must hand over all the 9s she has in her hand, but if she has none, she says, "Go Fish."

Then you draw the top card of the stock. The turn to ask then passes to the player to your left.

If you succeed in getting some cards when you ask for them, you keep your turn and may ask again. You may ask the same player or some different player, and you may ask for any rank in your new question.

If you have been told to "go fish" and you pick a card of the rank you just asked for, you show the card immediately before putting it in your hand, and your turn continues. (In some very strict games, your turn would continue only if the card you fished for completed a book for you.)

When you get the fourth card of a book, you show all four, place them on the table in front of you, and continue your turn.

If a player is left without cards, she may draw from the stock at her turn and ask for cards of the same rank as the one she has drawn. After the stock has been used up, a player who has no cards is out of the game.

The game is over when all thirteen books have been assembled. The player with the most books wins.

Tips

You can learn about your opponents' cards by noticing which cards they request and play during their turn.

Suppose John requests queens and gets one queen from Sarah. John does not put down a book of queens, but asks a new question and is told to "go fish." You now know that John held at least one queen to give him the right to ask for queens. He has received a queen, which gives him a total of either two or three queens.

In the same way, you know something else about a player's hand when he asks for a card and gets nothing at all.

For example, suppose John asks somebody for 8s and is told to go fish. You know that he must have at least one 8 in his hand.

Little by little, you can build up information about the cards the other players are holding. If you know that another player has queens but you have no queens yourself, the information does you no good. If you have a queen yourself, however, you are then allowed to ask for queens—and if you ask the right person because of the information you have, you may get as many as three queens and be able to put down an entire book in front of you!

Number of players: two or more

The Object of the Game

To avoid getting "stuck" with the last unpaired queen.

The Deal

Discard one queen from the pack before beginning this game. Deal one card at a time to each player, as far as the cards will go. It doesn't matter if they don't come out even.

The Play

Sort your cards and put aside, face down, all cards that you can pair—two by two. For example, you might put aside two kings, two queens, two 7s, and so on. If you have three queens and three jacks, you would be allowed to put two of them aside, but the third card would stay in your hand.

After each player has discarded his paired cards, the dealer presents her cards, fanned out but face down, to the player at her left. That player selects one card (blindly, since the hand is face down) and quickly examines it to see if it pairs with some card still in his hand. If so, he discards the pair. In any case, this player now fans his cards out and presents them face down to the player at his left.

This game continues, each player in turn presenting his hand, fanned out and face down, to the player to the left. Eventually, every card will be paired, except one of the queens. The player who is left with the odd queen at the end of the hand is the "Old Maid" or the "Odd One Out."

Whenever a player's last card is taken, he drops out. He can no longer be the "Old Maid" or the "Odd One Out."

Tips

Old Maid can be learned in about one minute, and nothing you can do will improve your chance of winning. The player stuck with an odd queen during the middle of the play usually looks worried and will often smile with relief if the player to his left selects the queen. If you keep alert, you can usually tell which player at the table has an odd queen as the play is going on.

If you have the odd queen, put it somewhere in the middle of your hand when you present it to the player at your left. Most players tend to pick a card from the middle rather than the ends. You can also choose the cards at the ends of the hand you are selecting from.

It isn't bad to get an odd queen toward the beginning of the play, for you will have many chances to get rid of it. It will then probably stay in some other player's hand or move only part of the way around the table.

WAR

Number of players: two

The Object of the Game
To win all the cards.

The Deal
Deal one card to each
player until the deck is
divided in two.

The Play
The players put their
stack of cards face down
in front of them and turn
up the top card at the
same time. The player
who has the higher of

the two turned-up cards wins both cards and puts them face down at the
bottom of his stack of cards. The king is the highest card, and the ace is the
lowest. The full rank of cards is:

Highest 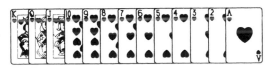 *Lowest*

Sometimes War is played with the ace high.

If the two turned-up cards are of the same rank, the players have a
"war." Each turns three cards face down and one card face up. The player
with the higher of the two new face-up cards takes both piles (a total of
ten cards).

If the newly turned-up cards again match, there is "double war." Each
player once again turns three cards face down and one card face up, and the
higher of these two new face-up cards wins the entire pile of eighteen cards.

The game continues until one player has all the cards.

This is a good game to play when you have a lot of time and nowhere
to go.

SNIP, SNAP, SNOREM

Number of players: three or more

The Object of the Game
To get rid of all your cards.

The Deal
Deal one card at a time to each player, until the pack is used up. It doesn't matter if some players have more cards than the others.

The Play
The player to the left of the dealer puts any card face up on the table. The next player to the left matches it with the same card in a different suit, saying "Snip."

The next player to the left matches the original card with the same card in a third suit, saying "Snap." The next player follows with the fourth card of the same kind, saying "Snorem." If a player is unable to follow with a matching card, he says "Pass," and his turn goes to the next player to the left.

Let's say that Allan puts down a 6 of hearts. The next player to the left, Bette, has no 6 and therefore must say "Pass." Carol, the next player, has the 6 of Diamonds and puts it down, saying "Snip." Dennis, the player to the left, has both of the remaining 6s and puts them down one at a time, saying "Snap" for one and "Snorem" for the other.

Then Dennis (the player who said "Snorem"), after putting down the fourth card of a kind, plays the first card of the next group of four. If he has more than one of a kind, he must put down as many as he has instead of holding out one of the cards for "Snorem."

For example, if you decide to put down kings, and you have two of them, you must put both of them down at the start. You're not allowed to put down just one of them and wait for the other two kings to appear before showing your remaining king for a "Snorem."

The first player to get rid of his cards wins the game.

SLAPJACK

Number of players: two to eight

"Slapjack" is one of the most entertaining games that you can play with a deck of cards.

The Object of the Game

To win all the cards.

The Deal

Deal one card at a time to each player until all the cards are dealt. It doesn't matter if they don't come out even. The players square up their cards into a neat pile face down in front of them without looking at any of the cards.

The Play

The player to the left of the dealer begins by lifting the top card of her pile and dropping it face up in the middle of the table. The next player (to the left of the first) does the same—lifts the top card of his pile and drops it face up in the middle of the table on top of the card that is already there.

The game continues in this way—until any player turns up a jack. Then the fun begins. The first player to slap that jack wins the entire pile of cards in the middle of the table! If more than one player slaps the jack, the one whose hand is at the bottom wins the pile.

This means that you have to keep your eyes open and be pretty quick to get your hand down on a jack. Sometimes another player slaps your hand instead of the jack, but it's all in fun.

I used to beat my grandfather because he would lift his hand high in the air before bringing it down on a jack, while I would swoop in sideways and snatch the jack away before his hand hit the table. Grandpa never seemed to learn!

When you win cards, put them face down underneath the cards you already have.

The play goes on until one player has won all the cards. As soon as a player has lost his last card, he may watch for the next jack and try to slap it in order to get a new pile for himself. If he fails to get that next pile, he is out of the game. Sooner or later, all the players except one are "knocked out," and the cards all come to one player, who is the winner.

False Slaps

A player who slaps at a card that is *not* a jack must give the top card of her pile to the owner of the card that she slapped. If the false slapper has no cards to pay the penalty, she is out.

How to Turn Cards

At your turn to play, you must lift the top card of your pile and turn it away from you as you drop it face up in the middle of the table. This is to make sure that you don't see the card before the other players do. Also, make sure that you let the card go as you drop it. Naturally, you don't want the other players to have a big advantage, so turn the card over very quickly. Then you will see it just about as soon as they do.

Tips

Most players use the same hand for turning the cards and for slapping at jacks. It's a more exciting game, however, if you agree that the hand used for slapping will not be the same hand used for turning the cards.

Some players use the right hand to turn over the card with a quick motion, and they swoop down on the jack with the left hand.

You may want to try it both ways to see which is better for you.

The important thing to remember is that it's better to be a swift swooper than a slow slapper.

I DOUBT IT

Number of players: three or more

When you have three or four players, use one deck of cards. When you are playing with five or more, shuffle two packs together.

The Object of the Game

To get rid of all your cards.

The Deal

Two or three cards at a time are dealt so that each player gets an equal number of cards. When only a few cards are left, deal one at a time as far as the cards will go.

The Play

The player to the dealer's left puts from one to four cards face down in the middle of the table, announcing that she is putting down that number of aces.

The next player puts down one to four cards and announces that he is putting down that number of 2s.

The next player in turn does the same thing, stating that he is putting down that number of 3s. And the play proceeds in this sequence:

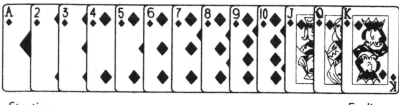

Starting   *Ending*

When any player puts down cards and makes his announcement, any other player may say, "I doubt it." The suspect cards must immediately be turned face up. If the statement was true, the doubter must take the entire pile into his hand. If the statement was false, the player who made the false statement must take the pile.

When you're using two packs shuffled together, a player may put down any number of cards, from one to eight.

When a player puts his last cards on the table, some other player must say, "I doubt it," since otherwise the game ends automatically. If the statement turns out to be true, the player wins the game.

A player who has no cards at all of the kind that she is supposed to put down is not allowed to skip her turn. She must put down one or more cards anyway and try to get away with her untruthful announcement. If somebody doubts her claim, she will have to pick up the pile.

If two or more people say, "I doubt it," at the same time, the one nearest the player's left wins the tie and must pick up the pile if the statement turns out to be true after all.

CRAZY EIGHTS

Number of players: two to eight

This game is best for two, three, or four players. In a four-handed game, the players who sit across the table from each other are partners.

The Object of the Game

To get rid of all your cards. The first player to get rid of them wins.

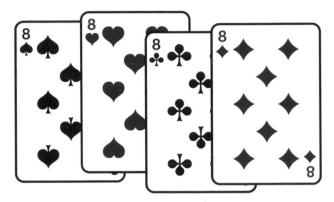

The Deal

Deal out seven cards to each player in a two-handed game, five to each player when more than two are playing.

Put the rest of the cards on the table face down as the stock. Turn the top card face up to begin another pile.

The Play

The player to the left of the dealer must match the card that has been turned up. That means he must put down a card of the same suit or of the same rank.

For example, suppose that the card first turned up is the 9 of spades. The first player needs to put down another spade or a 9. That card is placed on top of the turned-up card. It is up to the next player to match the new card either in suit or in rank.

The four 8s are wild, which means that you may play an 8 at any time when it is your turn. When putting down an 8, you are allowed to call it any suit at all, as you please.

For example, you might put down the 8 of hearts and say "spade." The next player would then have to follow with a spade.

If, at your turn, you cannot play, you must draw cards from the top of the stock until you are able to play or until there are no more cards left. You are allowed to draw cards from the stock at your turn, even if you are able to play without drawing. This is sometimes a good idea.

Sometimes a hand ends in a block, with nobody able to play, and with nobody having played out. The hand is then won by the player with the smallest number of cards. If two or more players tie for this honor, the hand is declared a tie.

Strategy

The most important principle is not to play an 8 too quickly. If you waste an 8 when you are not really in trouble, you won't have it to save you when the going gets tough.

The time that you really need an 8 to protect yourself is when you have been run out of a suit.

For example, after several spades have been played, you might not be able to get another spade, even if you drew every single card in the stock.

If you are also unable to match the rank of the card that has been put down, you may be forced to pick up the entire stock before your turn is over. From here on, of course, it will be very hard for you to avoid a disastrous defeat. An 8 will save you from this kind of misfortune, since you can put it down in place of a spade, and you may be able to call a suit that does for your opponent what the spade would have done for you.

If you're lucky, you won't have to play the 8 as your next to last card. It would be better to play it when your next turn comes—and win the hand. To play an 8 with more than two cards in your hand is seldom wise. It is usually a good idea to draw a few cards from stock in order to find a playable card.

Tip

The best way to beat an opponent is to run her out of some suit. If you have several cards in one suit, chances are your opponent will not have many. As often as you get the chance, keep coming back to your long suit, until your opponent is unable to match your card. Eventually, she will have to draw from stock and may have to load herself up badly before she is able to play.

BASIC RUMMY

Number of players: two to six

The Object of the Game

To win points from your opponents. To do this, you have to match up your cards by getting three or four of a kind, or sequences of cards that are next to each other in rank and the same in suit.

For example, you could match up three kings or four 10s, or a sequence of cards like:

Highest   *Lowest*

or

A typical sequence

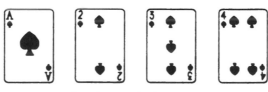

Another typical sequence

You need at least three cards for a sequence.

The Deal

Deal ten cards to each player when two are playing, seven cards to each when three or four are playing, and six cards to each person when five or six are playing.

Put the rest of the cards face down in the middle of the table, forming the stock. Turn the top card face up, starting the discard pile.

The Play

Each player at the table plays in turn, beginning with the player to the dealer's left. In your turn, you do three things:

> You draw a card from the stock.
>
> You meld, if you can.
>
> You discard.

When you draw, you may pick up the top card of the stock or the top card of the discard pile. You add this card to your hand.

To meld, you put a group of matched cards down on the table, if you are lucky enough to have three or four of a kind or of a sequence.

You don't have to put them down, though. You can keep them in your hand, if you want.

You can also, on your turn, add to any meld that is out on the table.

For example, if someone has put down three kings, you may add the fourth king when it is your turn to play. If someone has put down the 6, 7, and 8 of diamonds, you could add the 9 and 10 of diamonds, or the 5 and 4, or any such card or group of cards.

After you have drawn and melded—or after you have declined to meld—it is your turn to discard. You can take any card from your hand and put it on top of the face-up pile in the middle of the table. This completes your turn.

If, on your turn, you manage to meld all your cards, you win the game. You must begin your play with a draw, thus adding one card to your hand, and then you must meld either all the cards in your hand or all but one, which would be your discard.

If no player has melded all his cards (called "going out") by the time the stock is used up, the next player may take either the top card of the discard pile or the top card of the new stock that has been formed by turning the discard pile over. In either case, the game goes on as before, until somebody does go out.

Scoring

The winner of a hand scores points by counting up the hands of all the other players in the game. Each loser counts the cards in his hand according to the following scale:

Point Value of the Cards
Picture cards = ten points each
Aces = one point each
Other cards = face value

A loser does not count cards that he has previously melded on the table, but he does count any cards that remain in his hand—*even if these cards match!*

When you meld all your cards in one turn, without previously melding or adding to anybody else's meld, it is called "going Rummy." Whenever you "go Rummy," you win double the normal amount from each of the other players.

Keep score with pencil and paper, setting up a column for each player. Whenever a player wins a hand, put the amounts that he wins from the other players into his winning column.

Some players agree on a stopping time when they play Rummy. The winner is the player with the highest score when that time is up. Other players end a game when any player reaches a certain total score, such as 500 points. The score for each player is added up at the end of each hand.

Strategy

In all games of the Rummy family, you try to build up your hand by keeping cards that match and discarding cards that don't.

For example, if you drew the 10 of spades, you would tend to keep it if your hand contained one or more 10s, or the jack of spades or the 9 of spades. Even if it did not immediately give you a meld, it would probably bring you closer to one.

If you drew a card that didn't match anything in your hand, you would either discard it immediately or wait for a later chance to discard it.

If the player to your left picks up a card from the discard pile, this gives you a clue to what's in his hand. If, for example, he picks up the 9 of diamonds, you know that he must have other 9s or other diamonds in the neighborhood of the 9. If convenient, you might avoid throwing another 9 or another diamond in that vicinity onto the discard pile.

This is called "playing defensively." You don't need to bother with defensive play against anybody but the player to your left, since your discard would be covered up by the time any other player wanted to draw.

The advantage of melding is that you cannot lose the value of those cards, even if some other player wins the hand.

The advantage of holding a meld in your hand is that nobody can add to the meld while it is still in your hand. A second advantage is the possibility of "going Rummy" all in one play.

It sometimes pays to hold up a meld, but most successful Rummy players make it a habit to put melds down fairly quickly. It's usually safe to hold up a meld for one to two turns, but after that it's dangerous. If another player goes out before you have melded, you will lose those matched cards just as though they were unmatched.

Number of players: two to six

This is the basic and most simple of the Hearts family. It is almost always played with four people; if you have more players, other variants of the game are better.

You also need a handful of counters for this game—toothpicks, pebbles, dried beans, etc., the same number to each player—or paper and pencil.

The Object of the Game

To avoid winning any hearts—or to win all thirteen of them.

The Deal

Each player receives thirteen cards. When you can't divide them equally, remove enough 2s from the deck to make the deal come out even. Aces rank highest.

The Play

The player to the left of the dealer makes an opening lead and the cards are played in tricks. A trick is won by the highest card played of the suit led. The winner of the first trick also gets the leftover 2s, if any were taken out of the deck when dealt. These cards are called "widows." If you don't have a card in the trick suit, you can play any card in your hand. There is no trump suit, though hearts are often mistakenly called trumps. The winner of a trick leads the next trick.

Scoring with Counters

For each heart that a player wins, he must pay one counter into the pool.

If two or more players take no hearts, they divide the pool. But if all the players take hearts, nobody wins the pool. It stays on the table as a jackpot and becomes part of the pool for the next deal.

Scoring with Paper and Pencil

Each heart taken counts one point to the player. A game can be ended at any agreed-upon time, and the player with the lowest total score is the winner. If a player wins all the hearts, the usual method of scoring is to deduct thirteen from his score. Some people deduct double that—twenty six, instead.

KLONDIKE

Number of players: one

This is probably the most popular solitaire game in the world.

The Layout

Lay out seven cards in a row face down except for the first card. Then put the eighth card face up on the second card in the row, and complete the row with face down cards. Place a face-up card on the third pile, and finish off the row in the same way. Continue until you have a face-up card on every pile. Your layout will look like the diagram below.

The Object of the Game

Build up complete suits from ace to king.

The Play

First, look over the spread carefully. Move any cards that you can to the foundation row—aces and any cards you can build on them.

You can also build cards on the layout. Only face-up cards are available for building, and only if they are the exposed cards of the pile. Then you can build downward on them in alternating colors.

In the example shown here you can move the ace up to the foundation row, and then move the black 3 onto the red 4, and the red 2 onto the black 3.

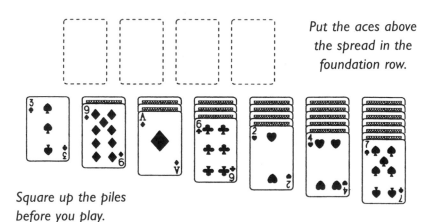

Put the aces above the spread in the foundation row.

Square up the piles before you play.

Every time you move a face-up card, you turn up the face-down card beneath it. When there are no more face-down cards in a pile, you have a space. Spaces can be filled by any available king.

When you've made all the moves you can, start going through the stockpile one by one, looking for more cards to build onto the foundations and the layout. If you can't place a card, it goes onto a wastepile; the top card of the wastepile is available for play.

Scoring

Five rounds make a game. Add up the number of foundation cards you come up with in each round for your final score.

GLOSSARY

Ante up. To put counters into the pool so that they may be won during the game.

Build. In solitaire, to place one card on another to create a sequence—whatever kind is called for. Usually, the sequence just goes up or down. The queen, for example, is placed on the king if the sequence is down, on the jack if it's up.

Capot. Trying to win all the tricks.

Column. Cards that go vertically in a line.

Deuce. 2s.

Discard pile. The pile of cards already played or rejected by the players.

Follow suit. Put down a card that matches the suit of the lead.

Foundations. The cards that score—the ones you build on in solitaire. They are usually—but not always—put up above the layout.

Lead. The first card that establishes the suit to follow.

Meld. To match up three or four cards of a kind or in sequence. Can be held in the hand or put down on the table. A matched set.

Rank. The number of a card. A 10 of diamonds "ranks" higher than a 9 of diamonds.

Revoke. Not following suit when you could have and were supposed to.

Row. Cards that go horizontally in a line.

Sequence. Three or four cards of a suit in order.

Set. Three or four cards of the same rank.

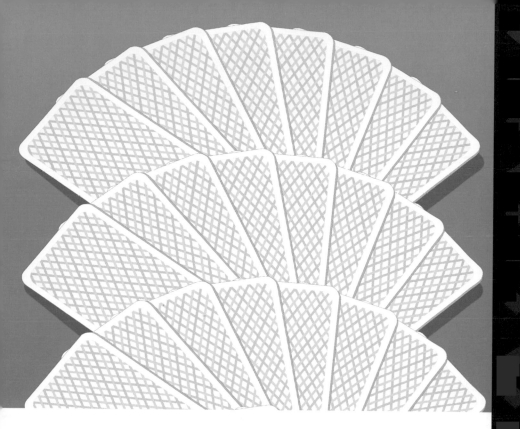

Stock. Unplayed cards (the pack) from which a player may draw a new card or from which the dealer may deal new cards to players.

Suits. Hearts, diamonds, clubs, and spades.

Trick. A sequence in which each person plays a card according to certain rules.

Trump suit. A named suit that can overtake others.

Up card. The top card of the stock, turned up to start the discard pile.

Waste pile. The discarded cards.

Widow. An extra hand or number of cards that may be substituted for a player's own hand or held until a certain point in the game. Also, extra cards taken with the first trick in hearts.

Wild cards. Cards that prior to the start of play may be given any value you choose.

INDEX